PLANT
DEFENSES

PLANTS THAT MOVE

MOLLY MACK

PowerKiDS
press

New York

Published in 2017 by The Rosen Publishing Group, Inc.
29 East 21st Street, New York, NY 10010

First Edition

Editor: Sarah Machajewski
Book Design: Reann Nye

Photo Credits: Cover Mariah Mariah/Shutterstock.com; p. 4 TunedIn by Westend61/Shutterstock.com; p. 5 (both images) Valerie Giles/Science Source/Getty Images; p. 6 Diana Taliun/Shutterstock.com; p. 7 MJ Prototype/Shutterstock.com; p. 8 picturepartners/Shutterstock.com; p. 9 Sue Robinson/Shutterstock.com; p. 10 Alvaro German Vilela/Shutterstock.com; p. 11 Westend61/Getty Images; p. 12 chatgunner/Shutterstock.com; p. 13 Joe Petersburger/National Geographic/Getty Images; p. 14 Kuttelvaserova Stuchelova/Shutterstock.com; p. 15 a9photo/Shutterstock.com; p. 16 Alex James Bramwell/Shutterstock.com; p. 17 AnastasiiaM/Shutterstock.com; p. 18 Warayoo/Shutterstock.com; p. 20 https://commons.wikimedia.org/wiki/File:StylidiumFlora5.jpg; p. 21 https://commons.wikimedia.org/wiki/File:Stylidium_turbinatum_column_movement.png; p. 22 nakorn/Shutterstock.com.

Cataloging-in-Publication Data

Names: Mack, Molly.
Title: Plants that move / Molly Mack.
Description: New York : PowerKids Press, 2017. | Series: Plant defenses | Includes index.
Identifiers: ISBN 9781499421477 (pbk.) | ISBN 9781499421491 (library bound) | ISBN 9781499421484 (6 pack)
Subjects: LCSH: Plants–Irritability and movements–Juvenile literature. | Climbing plants–Juvenile literature.
Classification: LCC QK771.M34 2017 | DDC 583'.04'18–d23

Manufactured in the United States of America

CPSIA Compliance Information: Batch #BS16PK: For Further Information contact Rosen Publishing, New York, New York at 1-800-237-9932

CONTENTS

WATCH OUT! 4

ADAPTATION
   SITUATION. 6

STAYING SAFE 8

MOVE IT!. 10

SO SENSITIVE 12

INSECT EATERS 14

CLIMBERS AND
   CREEPERS 16

CATAPULT!. 18

TRIGGER PLANTS 20

MOVING AND
   GROOVING. 22

GLOSSARY 23

INDEX 24

WEBSITES. 24

WATCH OUT!

Imagine playing basketball with your friends. Suddenly, the ball flies toward your head. Act fast! You could jump out of the way or block your head with your arms. Whatever you do, moving your body keeps you safe. Does it surprise you that some plants move to **protect** themselves, too?

Plants are rooted in the soil. However, some can move even though they're stuck in one place. They close their leaves or shrink when danger is near. And moving is used for more than just protection. Some plants climb to get sunlight and others move to catch food. Moving helps some plants survive. Let's learn more about it.

PLANT POINTER
A plant's ability to move is called motility.

The jewelweed's seed pods (above) explode
when they're touched (below), launching
seeds everywhere.

5

ADAPTATION SITUATION

Plants have been growing on Earth for millions of years. The goal of living **organisms** is to help their **species** survive to the next **generation**. Some plants have survived thanks to adaptations.

An adaptation is a change that helps an organism live in its **environment**. Movement is one kind of adaptation. Long ago, plants that were able to move survived longer than plants that couldn't. These moving plants lived to pass on their traits, while other plants were eaten or died out. Today, it's clear: these adaptations are the best way for some plants to survive.

PLANT POINTER

Different types of leaves are great examples of adaptations. Pine needles are leaves that have adapted to keep trees from losing too much water.

Adaptations appear in all kinds of plants and environments. Plants living near forest floors receive little sunlight. Some have adapted to these conditions by growing extra-large leaves to gather more light.

Living in the wild can be pretty **dangerous**. Plants face all kinds of **threats**. Animals and bugs want to eat them. People may pick them or cut them down. Even the weather can be dangerous to plants! Defenses are important adaptations that help organisms survive.

Plant defenses are really cool. Motility is just one example. Some plants give off a bad smell or pretend to look dead. The sharp spines on some plants tell us not to touch them. Some plants have oils or poisons that can really hurt us. These defenses do a good job of keeping predators away.

POISONOUS
BELLADONNA BERRIES

Deadly nightshade, or belladonna, is one of the most poisonous plants in the world! People know to stay away from it.

MOVE IT!

One major reason plants move is to get sunlight. This is called phototropism. This is when plants bend toward the light. If you want to see this in action, place a green plant in front of a window. It's sure to lean toward the window as time passes. It's trying to get sunlight so it can grow!

Plant movement can also be a response to something, such as being touched. Movements can be either really slow or really fast. For example, tree trunks can change the direction they grow based on **gravity**, but this takes a very long time. On the other hand, it takes just seconds for some plants to close their leaves around a bug.

TWISTED TREE TRUNK

This tree didn't let a stone building get in the way of surviving. Its roots simply moved around it.

SO SENSITIVE

The *Mimosa pudica* plant is sometimes called the **sensitive** plant. This is because of how it responds to being touched, shaken, or otherwise **disturbed**. In fact, it's so sensitive that its leaves close up when it's bothered!

Normally, the sensitive plant's leaves are filled with water, which makes them stiff and full. When the plant is touched, a reaction happens inside that makes water drain from cells at the base of the leaves. The leaves become limp and collapse! The leaves start folding just a couple of seconds after they're touched, but they open up again in 15 to 30 minutes.

PLANT POINTER

Mimosa pudica folds its leaves in response to touch, shaking, and strong winds. The leaves may even close due to heat or bright light.

The sensitive plant may fold its leaves to be less attractive to predators that would like to eat it. The folded leaves may look less healthy to predators.

INSECT EATERS

Bugs like to visit plants for dinner, but in some cases, the bugs may end up as dinner themselves! The Venus flytrap is a carnivorous plant, which means it eats bugs. First, it has to catch them.

Tiny hairs line the Venus flytrap's "mouth," which is actually a set of special leaves. When something brushes against the hairs—snap! The trap closes around the bug. The plant soon breaks down the bug's body, which becomes plant food.

Why do Venus flytraps move to catch their food? They commonly grow in poor soil, and eating bugs makes them healthier.

If the Venus flytrap couldn't move its leaves, it couldn't catch the food it needs to be healthy. It's a great example of how motility can help a plant survive.

CLIMBERS AND CREEPERS

Some plants climb walls, fences, and other tall objects—without arms or hands! Climbing plants, which are sometimes called vining plants, need to grow upward to get the most sunlight. However, their stems are weak and can't support the weight of the plant. Instead, the plants send out tiny stems called tendrils, which search for supports to hold on to.

Scientists think the tendrils "feel" around for supports. When they find a support, the plant sends a **signal** that tells the tendrils to latch on to it. Some tendrils coil, or curl, around a support. Some plants climb with parts that have hooks at the end.

PLANT POINTER
Cucumber tendrils shrink after they coil, which pulls the plant higher. Cool!

TENDRIL

Passionflower, cucumber, pea, and bean plants are common climbers.

CATAPULT!

Plants produce seeds and spores that make new plants when they're carried to other places. Bugs, animals, wind, and people help with this. However, some ferns have nothing to chance. They launch their spores like a **catapult**!

Ferns produce spores on the underside of their leaves. An annulus, or a row of thick, special cells, surrounds the spores. These cells shrink as they dry out. The shrinking pulls the annulus open, much like you would pull back the arm of a catapult. Suddenly, the annulus snaps back to its original shape! This throws the spores into the air.

PLANT POINTER
A spore is a tiny cell that can develop into a new plant. In some plants, spores act much like seeds.

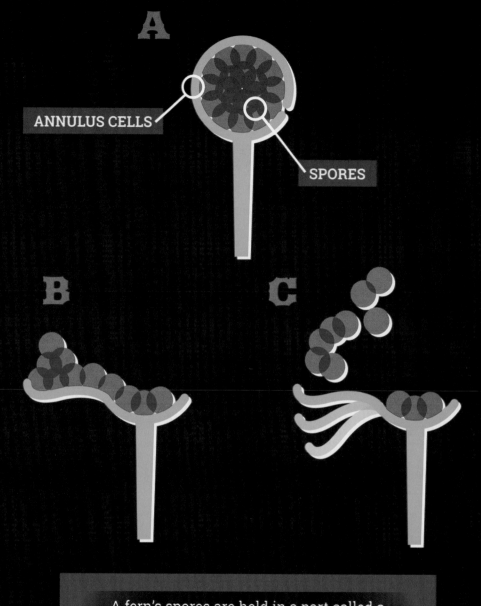

A fern's spores are held in a part called a sporangium, which also contains a row of cells called an annulus (A). The cells of the annulus shrink as they lose water, pulling the sporangium open (B). When the annulus snaps back to its original shape, the spores are launched into the air (C).

TRIGGER PLANTS

The hair-**trigger** flower, or trigger plant, is easy to recognize because of the part that gives it its name—the trigger! The flower has a trigger-like part that swings around when it's touched. This movement helps spread pollen, which helps the plant survive.

The process begins when a bug visits the flower. The trigger is still and covered with pollen. When the bug tries to drink nectar from the center of the flower, it sets off the trigger. This part snaps over the flower and releases its pollen all over the bug. The bug flies away, carrying the pollen with it. This pollen helps create new plants.

PLANT POINTER
The trigger plant's trigger doesn't hurt the bug, but the bug may be surprised!

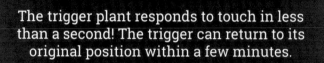

The trigger plant responds to touch in less than a second! The trigger can return to its original position within a few minutes.

MOVING AND GROOVING

Every plant is special in its own way, and many plant species are very different. However, the plants you've just read about have something cool in common—their ability to move.

Motility helps plants survive danger and stay safe from predators. It also helps plants face challenges, such as weak stems or poor soil. Perhaps most important, motility helps some plants spread pollen and spores, helping those species survive.

Plants that move come in all shapes, sizes, and colors. The next time you see a plant growing firmly in the ground, ask yourself: could it actually be on the move?

GLOSSARY

catapult: A military device that's used to throw large objects.

dangerous: Likely to cause harm.

disturb: To get in the way of how things normally are.

environment: The natural surroundings of a person, plant, or animal.

generation: All the plants that started growing about the same time.

gravity: The force that pulls objects toward the center of Earth.

organism: An individual plant or animal.

protect: To keep safe.

sensitive: Quick to respond to change.

signal: A message sent to produce an action.

species: A group of living organisms that have similar traits.

threat: Something that could cause harm.

trigger: Something that sets off a mechanism that produces an action.

INDEX

A

annulus, 18, 19

B

bean plants, 17
belladonna (deadly
    nightshade), 8, 9
bugs, 8, 10, 14, 18, 20

C

cucumber plants, 16, 17

F

fern, 18, 19

G

gravity, 10

J

jewelweed, 5

L

leaves, 4, 6, 7, 10, 12, 13,
    14, 15, 18

M

Mimosa pudica, 12, 13

P

passionflower plants, 17
pea plants, 17
phototropism, 10
pine needles, 6
pollen, 20, 22
predators, 8, 13, 22

S

seeds, 5 ,18
species, 6, 22
sporangium, 19
spores, 18, 19, 22
sunlight, 4, 7, 10, 16

T

tendrils, 16, 17
trigger plant , 20, 21

V

Venus flytrap, 14, 15

WEBSITES

Due to the changing nature of Internet links, PowerKids Press has developed an online list of websites related to the subject of this book. This site is updated regularly. Please use this link to access the list: www.powerkidslinks.com/plantd/move